AF251834

THE LIGHT ANGELS

For Jane,
Good friend in
writing and
appreciating —

Margaret Shipley
Dec. 4, 1988

THE LIGHT ANGELS

POEMS BY

Margaret Shipley

FITHIAN PRESS / SANTA BARBARA / 1988

Grateful acknowledgment is made to the following periodicals in which some of these poems were first published: *Blue Unicorn, Colorado Quarterly, Lyrical Iowa, Santa Barbara Independent, South Dakota Review, Spree, Texas Quarterly* (University of Texas Press, 1975), and *Western Humanities Review.*

The quotation for "Santorini" is from THERA by Christos G. Dumas, copyright ©1983 by Thames and Hudson Ltd. Reprinted by permission. The quotation for "Walking to December" is from Alastair Reid, "Visiting Lecturer," in WEATHERING, published by E.P. Dutton, New York, 1978. The quotation for *Venice* is from A LUME SPENTO by Ezra Pound, copyright ©1965 by New Directions Publishing Corp.

"The Old One" first appeared in THE EZRA POUND ANTHOLOGY, Wyndham Press, 1985. "Notes for a Greek Play" and "Salamis" first appeared in THE WRITING FINGER MOVES, An Anthology, Santa Barbara Writers Consortium, 1985.

LIBRARY OF CONGRESS CATALOG CARD NUMBER:
Shipley, Margaret.
    The light angels: poems / by Margaret Shipley — 1st ed.
    ISBN 0-931832-20-9 (pbk.) $7.50
    I. Title.
PS3569.H555L54   1989
811'.54—dc19   88-28730

Published by Fithian Press
Post Office Box 1525
Santa Barbara, California 93102

I tell you the story of lost in the woods,
the high stone window,
the fairy dressed as an old hag.

Someone alone in a far room
waits for the message. It arrives
by air, tied to the leg of a dove.

It says: Be patient. I am trying
to climb through the thorns to you.
If the hag knocks, don't let her in.

CONTENTS

1

Elise at the Keyboard   3
Spring Snow   4
Reflections in an Opaque Pond   5
Postcard from Colorado   6
A Perjury   7
Hypocrite Days   8
Poet as Hunter/One   9
Poet as Hunter/Two   10

2

A Camera in Rampur   13
Lantern Song   14
The Day I Stood Before the Winged
   Victory   15
Notes for a Greek Play   16
Catalpa   18
Salamis   19
A Longing for Islands   20
Slow Burn   21
Santorini   22
Picture Market: Haiti   24
Straw Market   25
Intimations of Travel   26
Risk   28

3

The Light Angels   31
Litany For a New House   33
Song of the Mountain Makers   34
Cemetery at Caribou   35
The Old One   36
The Swimmer   37
Kite on a Telephone Wire   38
Sundown Song   39
Ice Pond   40

4

Teal   43
Linnet   44
Dog Song   45
Junco   46
Egret Wading   47
Waterfall Bird   48

5

Girl Child   51
Tree, Child and Sun   52
Moment Before Class   54
The Academy Quarries Its Own Stone   55
Hommage to a Poet   56
Narcissus   57
Summer Recalled   58
Winter   59
Walking to December   60
Panning for Gold   62

1

ELISE AT THE KEYBOARD

3

From middle C her fingers run
into orchards of blossoming apple
where bees, brothers of the Navajo,
improvise themes begun Edens ago,
now run below the middle tone,
swim in water shine, leaf dapple,
wander into trout domain
into *allegreto, un poco vivace, crescendo*
wanting to strike at roots, I know—
return, saddened, to middle C again.

SPRING SNOW

We wait like stranded climbers
under the heavy cancellation,
all our wires down. No power.
Only the broadcasters have made it somehow.
Their voices rope us together:
Boy Scout circus called off,
bank closed, no busses running,
do not call in. Keep tuned, keep tuned.

Keep tuned to what the silence knows:
how the giant snow rising from the Gulf
with one sweep of his great glove
cancels clowns, wheels, money, our very foothold.
We drift to the window, give
him back his blank, innocent stare.

REFLECTIONS IN AN OPAQUE POND

5

Closed, unspeaking all forms: stones, pods, windows,
elms, roads, houses on this day nailed to the node
     of November.

Wrapped in the dreaming cone sleeps my lost
          astonishment,
my ill-remembered wonder lies under brown oblivion.

An age of leaves ago April a capella sang far, and I,
Eager listener, followed the wind, knew hunger

Sharp as minnow fin, awareness large as atmosphere.
Illusion turned to ember and to fall: the fever
          was ephemeral.

How lost are those green caprices of nymph, sprite,
          satyr, human,
is loudest of all the silences I sit and stare upon.

POSTCARD FROM COLORADO

This rockrimmed bowl they call
home: they have their own winds
that swirl around, around,
never leaving their walls,
their own sun that drinks their wells
like a madman. The people
hardly regret shade and moss
of east and south, their eyes
focus far to snows all year,
their motions are large.

Green grows in needled bunches
casting fat shadows, air
as thin as gauze filters light
deep into cliff crevass, dry grass.
We are never alone: so magnified
is this land in the round
convex lens of tall noon
we can touch that peak, that alpine field,
speak to each other much deeper
than face to face.

A PERJURY

A mile above the sea our snows fall
lightly, vanish under sun. By night
it tends to strain belief, perjure sight
to find the drifted flake ephemeral,
the jonquil pushing up—half a foot
of earth above a bulb is not enough,
it rises fooled unless that much and half
again is used and rises then in doubt,
as do we all, of winter where a snow
comes and goes at hide and seek with hot,
hare and pheasant track are there, are not,
hyacinth and willow wand show,
and rim of snow on window ledge at noon
by evening is forgot. It tends to break
the faith, a field by sundown going bleak
whose morning blaze of ice-reflected sun
struck amber, steel and jade from every stem,
fused with fire the poles of hot and cold
in flowers of light the mind may never hold
nor quite recall as noonday shatters them.

HYPOCRITE DAYS

THE HYPOCRITE DAYS . . . BRING DIADEMS
AND FAGOTS IN THEIR HANDS.
                    —RALPH WALDO EMERSON

I take this diadem for my crown
and set aside these fagots
the single-filed hours brought
who leaving their gift or curse
in my hands moved off-stage
with veiled faces into woods
where tomorrow is made.
Down-dropping blossoms rain
gold at my feet with no sound.
I shuffle through them thinking
of Danae who understood love
and how the minds of Concord
on the transcendental brink
foundered in greeds and railroads.
Now that our destiny is clear
having forgotten streams and ponds
nor remembered how to live our days
I wear each little crown an hour
and warm my hands at fagot fire.

POET AS HUNTER/ONE

Have never trapped doves
in a net at Béhorléguy,
have never shot shot
into a trip-hammer heart
or deciphered death
in stunned eyes
or held in hand bones
and feathers light
as willow leaf although
minutes ago they plummeted
leaden to earth.
But oh, I fling a mist net
every new day for you,
my bird, masked shrike
who perches out of range
then fires itself at glass,
cotton-winged owl who floats
soundless with open talons,
rain forest one who calls
first here, then there,
catch me if you can.
Illusive one, you lock all
language in your head.
You know your poor hunter
teased by the kill can never
quite zero in.

POET AS HUNTER/TWO

Ghost with broken horn
you appear from nowhere
the only brown shape
on my white field.
The spruce behind you
are dark with perplexity
where I have dared go.
Now you come to light.
You expect me to speak
or shout or sing.
You know me: I'm the one
With the arrow, the gun.
You've left me standing
in more than one wood
wishing for blood.
If you are ghost of the one
I shot, forgive.
I dream the broken prong,
the red drop.
If you are double and I
must sing to you again,
stay dark, sweet brown.

2

A CAMERA IN RAMPUR

Slight figures in transparent saris
trail saffron in the light wind
and wild strawberry stain in the sun,
advance in a row erect as eucalyptus
bearing water jars, their brown heads
proud as geese, their long hair
pliant as grass, advance in a shy dance.

They come from the river with no music,
only the hum of noon where boys
the color of soil argue in the dust,
girls bend under the burden of girlhood,
old men stare down the ghost, and peafowl
scream at the blue jay. That day
stops forever as the water bearers come
out of the river into the eye of my praise.

LANTERN SONG

Mei Ling sits where quince blossoms
    drop like lighted rain.
She feels a dazzle on her skin.
Oriental, the name for her world,
    is the lantern she floats in.

Tiny gardens, austere stones and bridges
    are not for her however.
She is a student of bio-chem at Michigan
with a minor in fine arts. She has seen
    wings hover.

She stares at her luminous arms,
listens to beating feathers over her.
Her lantern sways in drenched blossoms.

When I am a thousand years old
    thinks Mei Ling
I shall still be young. My body
    is burning stone.
It is stone on fire whether still
    or dancing.
My shadow is a bird lighter than air.

She has never heard of time's chariot
    hurrying near. Even so
her lantern is chosen to swing
free in raining quince for one evening.

THE DAY I STOOD BEFORE
THE WINGED VICTORY

In the gallery corridor
I saw the spirit in the stone
the shape occur
of time dressed in air
body of fire set free
in one long stroke

Dante heard the mastersong
begun by Daniel
but in Aquinas
wrapped in his dark face

So I have walked many rings
one below another since then
pondering the moment
I heard the angel sing
in stone in my own time
found a trace of unicorn

What light   what grace
preserves that form
of pure Orient   Greek phrase
on my eyelids now
only the shape of that day
can contain

NOTES FOR A GREEK PLAY

ACT ONE

After the fisher's caique left us
on the west shore of Aegina to picnic
we ate wild garlic in fun and crawled in pain,
dug our nails in driftwood and in rock,
our hands shriveled as Tutankhamon's neck.
A curlew or some Greek waterbird laughed
at our shame, demanded sick young entrails
in sacrifice. We gave him the shine of that Aegean
day, left our childhood in his nesting cave.

ACT TWO

Those prawns we drew in nets from pools
at Vouliagmeni—such flesh, all Neptune's doing,
outplumps a baby's thumb. Time held us at bay
there beside the waves, green coastal wake
of yachts. You said you saw a hitchhiker
with a trident break the sea and yell:
Your lives are museum artifacts,
Come, draw the net for octopus and eel!

ACT THREE

All hurt return to Hellas. So exiles come
To Tatoi, palace of the king. Only iron
Russian bells have withstood the Hun.
Too cumbersome to cry, they hang dumb
in pines over Alexander's tomb. I, outcast

on history's dry estate, peer in windows
where a queen once cried and combed her hair.
The wind in Tatoi's trees sings:
Stasis I love you more than ecstasis
but in ecstasis all bells ring.

CATALPA

Kanari Street drinks their shade alive.
What do they sing to our city,
choirs of heads with wings?
The trumpets of silence are loud.
The sphinx grub feeds and changes
in that Asiatic dark the Greeks
named *kutuhlpa*. The hawk moth
flies unconscious out of the worm.
Here in Kanari Street I think
of the angered Turk, the ignorant Hun
and all folk who went on singing
gripped in the fist of change
whose songs went down unheard.
Still the cutulpa-sphinx consumes
our green shade and changes form.
The Greeks looked, and went on, warned.

SALAMIS

The island lies out there, a lioness
breathing blue Aegean sunlight
knowing what she knows of sunken Persian ships:
she sings of drowned sailors.

Those alive there comb her sides
with strong brown fingers trained to twist
her hemp for netting fish or bagging grapes
and olives the size of girls' eyes.

The history Salamis sings leaves a shine
on her cockled fur I begin to comprehend
as I hear her litany escape the rotten hulls
off her eastern flank: out of the ribs
of Xerxes' ships an idea once hit the sun:
demokratia occurred to Athens.

A LONGING FOR ISLANDS

Goat bells, a pale sky
pull me to Skyros,
accordion in Tinos calls my tune,
whenever wind-sails whirl in Mykonos
I burn.

Sounion's temple anchored to the rock
reduces me to hunger in the bone,
not to climb Nike, not to cross
broken courts of wind-smooth stone
is loss.

Folded sails will never catch my ease
or tangled nets renew me as I go—
until I eat the honey-bitter olive
of the Cyclades, I neither sorrow
nor love.

SLOW BURN

You male sun
boss of my days
hot lover too brash
for my white skin
married to saronged
brown-skinned dancers
in south ocean islands,
copper coin, gong
medal of honor hung
on the royal blue robe of space—
all these years how to
return your brass stare
has been my embarrassment.
You won't let me look at you
but you blind me with your gold eye,
glare into my windows
dry my bread
bleach my hair
run me into shade
on a summer day.
We do communicate:
long ago you chose me
by a warm touch on a beach.
I stretched and sighed
I love you, Sun, I love you.
Do you hear me?
Or enraged at mere words
do you mean to burn me?

SANTORINI

*TIME STOOD STILL ON THAT SUMMER DAY
WHEN THE FIRST LAPILLI OF PUMICE FELL.*
—CHRISTOS DUMAS, *Thera*

When the pungent lapilli first fell
that summer bronze-age day at Akrotiri
a girl's hand must have followed down
this nippled ewer made by her father
(we know it is local by absence
of mica in the clay) to drop in her lap:

> I should flee but on my wall
> swallows fly among lilies
> without moving a feather. Every spring
> there's a rising of petals and wings.
> I will be alive like them.

Ash drift silvers her Minoan dress,
her skin is overlaid with pearl.

> I will be statued here in pumice.
> Antelope, puma, panther, lion, bull
> will pose in stone around me.
> Children will pommel my arms for joy
> because I am still beautiful.
> When the last fragrant lapilli fall

and I sit sixty meters deep
held fast among my father's amphorae
I'll be alive as flowers and swallows are.

Time pared her to volcanic grit, snuffed
her, breath by dusty breath, yet
her antique spirit outflies the swallows,
invisible

PICTURE MARKET: HAITI

His green is greener than lichen, moss, slime
    or imagined gem, elemental
    as a child's text of Dick and Jane.
His blue does not exist in nature or in the tube
    but must have boiled up into his eyes
    out of wells of bewilderment and lies.
He sees the narrow stream as zigzag,
    all elbows, angles, hard as ice
    in this tropic field where water never ran
    so obdurate as his unflexed determination.
      Ah, the grasses—
    each blade delineated
    with fanatic care
    as if a fear of generalities
    (to see the forest not the trees)
    would unveil the horrid truth
    of himself lost in a horde of poor.
Those brown bumps bent among the grasses
    so low they have no heads or faces
    are not mud clods, he means, but laborers.
The crop they cut is his secret. Here alone
    the painter is imprecise. How to design man
    in a world where water is stiff, grass stands alone,
    sky and growth are aesthetically monstrous
    only a god could figure out. He is human.
He paints his gross illusion the best he can.

STRAW MARKET

Port Au Prince, Haiti

Under the great tent
men in red shirts
women in flowers
sell straw:
straw baskets, straw hats,
straw Christ on a stick.

Children with muddy heads
sweep up the dirt.
Their arms and legs are broomsticks
stained by Caribbean sun.
A man coughs a string of fear.
His mouth goes dark red.

Uphill from the market
artists walk on woven soles,
mothers and fathers
cut bamboo day after day.
I buy a palm-leaf hat
to forget the lip-cracking sun.

What the sun grows and dries
is cloth and roof for these bodies
alive on this poor earth.
A lone straw in a man's mouth
takes on the look of hope.

INTIMATIONS OF TRAVEL

Meknès

Arabs in the Meknès medina:
canvas roofs stripe them bronze and gold,
each burnous floats luminous in oil air,
copper and leather sound, olive taste.
We finger silver lace, metal-throated gong.
The cadi bows low, the meuzzin cries
Come to the rancid East and be lost!

Our clothes once weightless
that loved to float in sunlight
drag now on our bodies,
we drowse in the hot shadows.
Under an awning in Oran
I remember the yellow dress you wore
drawing saffron off the sun.

Bélesta

A flake of bone from St. Anthony's knee
(*Honi soit Antoine!* the people sing)
peered like a pale face from the breast
of his likeness borne head-high and windowed
at Toussaint through the stones of Bélesta.
The crooked hands that crowned those oxen's ears
with buttercup, with wort, were not ours:
we waved the saints along unstained by death
that day, we thought, in the Langue d'Oc.

Venice

FOR I HAVE SEEN THE SHADOW
OF THIS THY VENICE.
> —A LUMA SPENTO

Above dank water and below it
loggias of the dead doges swim,
Byzantine arch, mosaic campanile
logged in rotten piles below ground,
mossed by tides above—a heavy tale
of piracy and commerce, striped sail,
poisoned love. Water to water runs:
the rain.
     In that wet romantic ghetto
east of businessman's Milan
tourist voices swim in red wine,
run sour, pour from every sewer.
We stand in the mash of Venezia's
old San Marco to our ankles in flood,
handle linens in shops, buy green glass.
Our hands shake, candles are lit,
people pray, bells toll. The shape
of a drowned child (is it a child?)
bumps the gondola pole,
straw head rolls, mouth sobs.

RISK

*A parachutist jumped from the observation
deck of the World Trade Center Saturday—UPI*

Some take long trips to the Bosporus
or Indrapuri never to return
or return and tell nothing.
Others deepsea dive then run off
in a wetsuit to avoid the press.
Others airdive or risk their bodies
on other bodies
never asking what they feel.

You and I know the rules: earth
draws courage or stupidity to itself
in a mix of concrete and glass.
Whatever falls breaks or walks away
sweetened by death or the media.
I looked up, saw you falling
toward me splendid in red
although red is not your color
and we love hungrier than before.

3

THE LIGHT ANGELS

Trapped in the towers of San Xavier, Tucson

Caroling full quietly they sing
hair all expanded dancing
    so light their bodies float
    their heads bump the roof
and richly laugh all silent.

Can be heard with simple non-ears
wrangling unheard bells
there in their high stone prison
a flock of tropical birds
themselves feathered sun
all luminous yet contained—
like love in the body's hold
warble in the flicker's throat
or under the lantern hood
intelligence with eyes, emerging

    and burn until dusk
    then softly snuff their light.
    Still their voices, flutterings
    whisper joy in their sleep.

Sweet Jesu that sleep
is the dropping of a warm snow
over those night towers.

All herbs become stars.
Their breathing washes the joshua shadows
with winds that overflow
the desert's deep stone jar.

LITANY FOR A NEW HOUSE

for Ann

Adobe walls are up, vigas are laid
let comfort fill this house

Let time interweave these rooms
as basket makers of Pecos weave
the bear grass and willow

May a good light rest on this roof
after rain

If Chinook trouble these walls
may they remain firm

May garden be green as peach-leaf dye
or dye of cedar bark

If blue spruce hum a new song
let it enter by these windows

Let oriole return to these eaves
Orion blaze on this chimney

By summer solstice may this house
be grown to the ground
old and warm for moons of snow

SONG OF THE MOUNTAIN MAKERS

Hear my song of laccolith,
Lyre and zither count the tale
Of burned stone in motion now,
Poem of powers primeval.

> *Ocean interloper, come,*
> *Blue marine millenium!*

Richly ored in granite stock
Rise the Rockies to their knees,
Mass Pre-Cambrian to meet
Mingled metamorphoses.

> *Down uptilted land unloose*
> *Tides, O Late Cretaceous!*

High on lava-fractured range
Rides the glacier, changing stream
Cuts the canyon to the plain;
Cirque remains, morainal dam.

> *Where ocean was, sands follow;*
> *Leave, O sea, your fossils now!*

Go, bard, to Niobrara,
Sing, harp, of Gunbarrel Hill;
Music's monument to stone
Be my only madrigal.

> *Linger, lakes of Laramie,*
> *Coal shall be your gift, O sea!*

CEMETERY AT CARIBOU

They came looking for a palace
of ore, found winds as rough
as a miner's beard, laced with ice.
Fevers ran their children
into the ground. Surprised,
they lie like sticks in rows,
their cries stopped by humus of fir.

Years deepened the aspen leaf,
shone through wintered skin,
swept the mountain timber-clean.
We bend over their strict bones:
their plots are small, their doubts
well resolved, their story told
by tundra and the high horizon.

THE OLD ONE

When the coyote
howled
he was my voice

When the prairie rang
my blood tipped
its bells

Something tied my body
to animals and water
those nights my breasts grew

I had no thought of death
or ever looked
at a lettered stone

or knew a wind
can cut a life loose
from solid things

Now I suck the wind
into my flute bones
and teach the owls

my tune. I stare
into their moon eyes
hearing *welcome welcome*

THE SWIMMER

Old memory and overall melt
of all that is metal, hard, littered,
this water is and is not. I am
and I am not. Into its cool lap
my upright rig of ligaments and bones
fell headlong shedding flesh on the way.
I am nothing exploring nothing.

No matter what palmful I scoop of it,
how far I dribble its lighted string,
wherever I press the face I used to have,
its coagulation moves away, it ignores
my forgotten body in its rush to unform.
I cannot rumple its tension to stay;
it reverts, recoups, reassembles.

What I must learn for sake of the mind I kept
when arms and legs dissolved is what
race of spirit I am involved in. I reach
for its essence with every stroke, kick up a froth
with nonfeet for a glitter of the truth.
Rage as I might to be someone in its eyes
water closes on itself where I was.

KITE ON A TELEPHONE WIRE

Leonardo in his imaginings
of what had not yet flown,
trying this shape and that
in the mild Florentine air
to prove the poetry of motion
to a world carved in stone,
of all men to understand
the time-lapse of the mind
might have recognized this
for what it is: tissue and balsa
pitched by downdraft to hang
torn on the trace of our voices
flying from city to city
and might have seen clear
the meaning of our sounds.

SUNDOWN SONG

Raw omens gang in cloud
more blood than fog,
mute as unrung iron bells.
Shadows veer across, black:
a Hitchcock flock of crows
scores the wires, dark measure.
Now they caw.
Against the sky in chaos
they speak in runes, spells.

My body is caught alone
in this conundrum.
I am young, bound
in an old cloth.

Whether clouds or crows
will take me over
no need to wonder.
One by one they go
beyond me into storybook,
leave a rumor
of trombones, drums
in my lungs, my bones.

A full moon rolls me home.

ICE POND

This Breughel scene on which
a random plan of people
moves in painter's fives and threes,
true to Dutch blues and reds, even to
Auden's ignored disaster (a child
is down under heedless blades)
this framed work has other news
for us than figure eight, whirled
girl, scratched wake: flesh
and wool, warmth and pitched voices
take shape in the cool vapor
by cleaner definition, purer art
than those of the Flemish masters,
as a poem at the same cost will fall
wide of the pond it would plunder.

4

TEAL

43

Smoke-shot, his atmosphere once purple
Blue and lovely becomes dangerous.
He, adaptable to rain and ruin
In the marsh, cannot conform to shot.

Aware of spring before it greens,
Great in his gift to follow summer,
Knowing frost before the pampas blooms,
He has a single fault, being wild:
Shot from a blind, he dies.

LINNET

A new structure altogether yet
older than we are, we are told,
is this comic little linnet caught
from the vine: utter bone and air, free
when let go. Thrills a crooked claw
across its beak, looks pure
panic at me, knows me well
for human, casual and able to hold
in my hand his breath, lord of a law
of lazy power that can crush.
The truth rings me like a bell,
plainer than his fear: his wizard skull
contains all, and I can only kill.

DOG SONG

He sprawls by the rose
dogstar over him
breathes in unison
with its orange heart
Dark climbs up from earth
down from cloud
wraps him in rose

Its glow doubles
in his drifting eye
His copper coat
older than rose leaves
gives its age to dusk
The blown rose leaps
on fire at his side

flickers on the edge of death
He prolongs his ease
held by the rose's dance
of impermanence
in his dogday wisdom
closes his eyes
as the rose dies

JUNCO

A while ago in deep pine shadow
his cloaked head and breast
masqueraded as shade, rosy sides
and white underneath disguised
themselves as patches of sun.
Now his undulating flight
works as a fitting together
of the two halves we thought
were not bird but light and dark.

Only in open spaces, his motion
seems to say, the bird may be seen
whole—as if a fragmentation
must occur in all forms designed
light and dark who sit in shadow,
and oneness achieved only where truth
meets the eye uncompromised.

EGRET WADING

I dream this bird, this ocean,
pity any spared the twist of awe
who go ungifted to a sleep
where no egret, slim dancer,
shimmers before their eyes,
no marbled waters rise
to rinse their feet, who wake
unchanged.

Given a glance at heaven
I live twice: first in body
to search and find, then
in spirit to feel and know.
Invisible I run my fingers down
the stately neck, stroke
the feathered crest, say Hello
to such beauty, praise the light
we see by, an egret wading.

WATERFALL BIRD

The ouzel (cinclus Mexicanus) dances
in Sierra spray. Waterproof water thrush
he whirls like a leaf in foam.
Hummingbird of waters, he sings
in the whisper and boom, gleans
his dinner of larvae in his bell glass
of deflected current, flies under water
on crisp wings, his feet unwebbed,
never flies overland but along
crooked streams, traces their windings.
Born on brink or snag, his first sight
of day is through a rainbow.

5

GIRL CHILD

She sleeps in the brilliant phase
of Jupiter. All her lines are praise,
appearing on our darkness as the least
foreseen of heavenly bodies and the most
illegible. We can only mark her eyes
as unknown suns on our sky, surmise
those signals from her dim continuum
faint rhythms of some living poem
not yet identified, fix in the air
an orbit for that dreaming sphere,
note the laws of light on her hair.

Still her name and number are untold.
We have studied how her shape will hold
the pattern sleeping of the Pleiades
from crown to nape to pelvic brink to knees,
how her nights are ringed in silk and soon
will fasten to the moorings of the moon—
and read one rule in her celestial pose:
the mystery that from her being glows
most unresolved, most marvelous.

TREE, CHILD AND SUN

Liquid elision from leaf
To leaf implies a slow deliquium
At heart, but willow of the veils lives a green life,
Provides a green room,

Cool curia for a child
Wise enough to rule her diocese
From a tree dome, annulate with native ease
Sparrows and friends in her hold.

Autumn in a snow
Rings in another scene: now cupric leaves
Drip a copper screen around her cold hollow,
Declension of dark in sheaves

Of light, brass curfew rung
On summer. Before dusk in the afternoon
She will see October sun withheld to burn on one
Tree: candelabrum, gong,

Buccinal sound of fall,
Shape of wild elk trumpet, cloud flame,
Sunset change, such sight empyreal to tame
Wilder than she, than all

Her animal domain,
Grand degringolade of tree and year
To simmering winter, smoke and sleep. And this rain
In falling rings her hair:

O bright anthelion
To praise her there as she rewards her tree
With medal stare, willow and child anomaly
Under a common sun.

MOMENT BEFORE CLASS

They are in that acre of awareness
before entering the wood. The girls' hair
swings, symbol of want. The boys watch
only their own kind, but hear the wind.

What they wear, how they speak
about each other's fears, where they make
their peace with truth, in what chapel
prey upon themselves, are the brunt

of the moment. The wood will swallow
all this, tie them with lines and angles,
numbers and laws. They'll see the underside
of leaves, they'll live on green geometric
verticals and planes, grow with the grain.
And exit the other side, cured of youth.

THE ACADEMY QUARRIES
ITS OWN STONE

If they seem eager to engage their books untroubled
by sighs of the ages in their ears, bend smooth
heads, illusive smiles over their lighted
pages, these boys and girls of the golden age,
it is because they do not understand standstone.
Oh they know it is there, a veneer for walls
they learn and live in, may even have written home
(the ones who know) *The academy quarries its own stone.*
If it does not disturb them, being closed in layers
of primordial ocean floor, or jar them out of youth
into scared mortality, it is because in their search
among Greeks for truth, equations for answers,
they overlook their fix: being flesh and new
where preadamic surge and sift of tide and deep
sigh *never, always, never* loud in library halls,
soft around the walls of their sleep.

HOMMAGE TO A POET

For a minute he tried to tell us
what it's like to be alive.
He sang it, prayed it, talked it,
wept it, wrote it by night light
into the folds of our clothes.

On a fair day of grass and sea
spiced with wings and pollen
I hear in the wind his praise of roses,
how opening and closing sea scrolls turn
him outside himself into fish, dolphin.

He took the rhythm of his heart for tide,
waded the shallows of his thin despair
day after day in a darkened room.
Now the sky embraces him.

Dear friend, singer of give and implore,
I come to the place of his repose
to study again his brief, red clamor.

NARCISSUS

If he had drowned
in his own eyes
as he wanted to
who can say what
he might have found
down there?

Twin stars fused
to twin stars
his body though lost
bound to his reflection

Double person yet one
so much in love
with himself
even Echo
can't make him hear

So intensely himself
under that surface
the unattainable attained
who can deny he invented
a new slant on death?

SUMMER RECALLED

Coming up over a hill
did you smell clover, ever?
A warm sun, a wind will
bring you the heady odor
like a bride brought by her lover
over the door sill. Remember
the richness of clover—
it is the day's kiss.

When summer is over
it can be tasted still
if recalled in quietness:
it hovers in fresh linen,
lives in the winter sun's caress
on window glass, may return in
a breath, a fever, a river
of aroma, wrapping you a moment
in waywardness.

WINTER

The evening turns copper
that once was coral.
In a rubble of stones
a snake glides to cover.

No warm flare of bloom
we know will come again
along the field's border
or collect in a shaded room.

Chastened by prick of winter
olive reveals a skeleton
clean of voluptuous leaf
as our scaffold love.

The air goes metallic.
We live where a north wind sings
high in monastic corridors
of snows in the marrow bone.

WALKING TO DECEMBER

TIME TELLS ITSELF THROUGH
SPELLS AND SUDDEN ORACLES.

—ALASTAIR REID

Spin the earth, April,
dizzy the vandals who broke branches
all winter in the elm. Chain the ankles
of the ice ghost who ridiculed the miracle
of water into wine. Throw pollen in the eyes

of critics who do not believe in flowers.
I wait to plunge my trowel into June.
For this I need a head for magic, to hear
the gong struck, bloodwhisper blaze into summer
when erotic Sun, my lover, takes over.

First, your rain. Your liquid shock
pommels rising bulb. Now explodes your leaf,
your terrible weed that fractures stone.
Old Mocker, astride his twig of magnolia,
lectures us all on lust. We listen.
Now you star the grass with bloom,
fling a cocktail party of small talk
all chattered in yellow buttercup, toss
lights into the wind, each torn bit
a tiny sun to burn out winter sin.

A crash of brilliance—August. As Paul
stood slapped, then wakened to track
the gold wire at last to Antioch, so I gape
at you, Sun, to the point of sleep, then dare
look into the boiling pit of your flowers,
lift their drug to my mouth. You give
me one more summer to carry the word
out of Damascus, to shake off the dust of Africa
via the Greeks and a ribbon of herons
over India. You give me stones in my shoe,
thorns in my sleeve—now feed me surfeit
of flowers, Sun, on the road to December.

Arctica, you wake in the north wind.
I feel your electric wing fan my hair.
If I flinch by reason of dregs of summer
in the blood, forgive, Great Splinterer.
Ignite if you must your brittle lightning,
thunder my self and my breath apart
but do it blindingly in one assault.
And be gentle with my self newborn.

PANNING FOR GOLD

62

Sometimes from the pan of dross
swirled out grain by grain
by the rhythms of your arms
you see a single shine,
its company of sand
washed away
by your circling will
to leave a wink of light,
an ore, a luck stone
and you believe again
in the bright unknown.

This book is composed in the type style designed by John Baskerville, an eighteenth-century designer of type and books, and manufacturer of paper and printing techniques.

Composed by:
Jim Cook/Book Design & Typography
Santa Barbara, California

Printed and bound by:
McNaughton & Gunn Lithographers
Ann Arbor, Michigan

Cover Art: Laure Dimston Spiers

ABOUT THE AUTHOR

Margaret Shipley grew up in Pasadena, California. Her first chapbook of poems, *The Root and the Leaf,* won the Durham Award for publication by American Weave. Her volume of poems, *Burning the Trees,* was published in 1985. She is the author of the novel, *The Sound of the Sun.* A number of her poems and short stories received the Tophand Award from the Colorado Author's League. Until recently she was a writer and editor at the University of Colorado in Boulder. She now makes her home in Santa Barbara, California.